Belles

OF THE
BALLPARK

Belles of the Ballpark

DIANA STAR HELMER

The Millbrook Press • Brookfield, Connecticut

Library of Congress Cataloging-in-Publication Data
Helmer, Diana Star, 1962–
Belles of the ballpark / by Diana Star Helmer.
p. cm.
Includes bibliographical references (p.   ) and index.
Summary: Describes the All-American Girls Professional Baseball
League, which gave women the opportunity to play professional
baseball while America was involved in World War II.
ISBN 1-56294-230-1 (lib. bdg.)
1. All-American Girls Professional Baseball League—History—
Juvenile literature.   2. Baseball—United States—History—Juvenile
literature. [1. All-American Girls Professional Baseball League—
History. 2. Baseball—History.] I. Title.
GV875.A56H45   1993
796.357'64'0973—dc20   92-12683   CIP   AC

Published by The Millbrook Press
2 Old New Milford Road
Brookfield, Connecticut 06804

CONTENTS

To everyone who gave to this work with a free heart.
There are many great hearts in this world.

And to Tom, who proves the above every day.

dh

One

TAKING
THE FIELD

America was at war. Pearl Harbor had been attacked on December 7, 1941. More bombings were feared; Americans prepared for attacks on the mainland. Citizens wondered if there would be enough to eat when soldiers needed food, or if there would be a way to travel when army tanks needed gasoline.

Safety, food, and gasoline filled the thoughts of most Americans in 1942. Philip K. Wrigley wondered: What about baseball?

Wrigley owned the Chicago Cubs baseball team. Would the game end, he wondered, when American men were gone to war? Wrigley thought, too, about his chewing gum factories. What would be made there when the world needed guns more than gum?

Wrigley's questions were valid, for the war occupied every aspect of American life. Homemakers saved cooking fats to help make bullets. Men who could not fight helped to recycle metals and rubber for military machines. Celebrities sold war bonds and entertained troops. Department stores stopped selling hosiery because the fiber they were made of was needed for parachutes; clerks were hired to mend old stockings for fashion-conscious customers.

Wrigley suspected that he could sell his peacetime products with patriotism. So he directed his gum-tree tappers to also tap rubber trees for the war effort. He voluntarily stopped wrapping his gum in foil, so the aluminum could be used for war industries. He sent free chewing gum to the soldiers. His patriotism was applauded, and the home front kept buying Wrigley's gum.

But baseball was a bigger challenge. More than half of all major-league players had signed with the military, leaving their old teams starless. Fans had trouble getting to ballparks, because gasoline was rationed and saved for the troops.

Baseball should just be canceled until the war's end, decided baseball commissioner Judge Kenesaw Mountain Landis. He wrote to President Franklin Delano Roosevelt for advice. Roosevelt's reply was written on January 16, 1942, just forty days after the bombing of Pearl Harbor.

My dear Judge:
Thank you for yours of Jan. 14. As you will, of course, realize, the final decision about the baseball season must rest with you and the baseball club owners. So, what I am going to say is solely a personal and not an official point of view.

I honestly feel that it would be best for the country to keep baseball going. There will be fewer people unemployed and everybody will work longer hours and harder than ever before.

And that means that they ought to have a chance for recreation and for taking their minds off their work even more than before.

Baseball provides a recreation which does not last over two hours or two hours and a half, and which can be got for very little cost. And, incidentally, I hope that night games can be extended because it gives an opportunity to the day shift to see a game occasionally.

As to the players themselves, I know you agree with me that individual players who are of active military or naval age should go, without question, into the services. Even if the actual quality of the teams is lowered by the greater use of older players, this will not dampen the popularity of the sport. . . .

Here is another way of looking at it—if 300 teams use 5,000 or 6,000 players, these players are a definite recreational asset to at least 20,000,000 of their fellow citizens—and that in my judgment is thoroughly worthwhile.

With every best wish,

Very sincerely yours,
Franklin D. Roosevelt

The president's approval was especially meaningful in 1942, when Roosevelt was serving an unprecedented third term. His popularity came from his swift action against the economic Depression of the 1930s. During those dark days, Roosevelt had become the first president to make regular use of the radio, talking to the public every week. He had been the first to open Oval Office doors and invite reporters in. His candor had won the public's trust.

Roosevelt fought unemployment during the Depression by creating new jobs. Now the war fought unemployment, too. Working men left the country to fight overseas just when factories needed them for around-the-clock war production. Typewriter manufacturers began making guns. Soda-pop companies bottled explosives instead. Where pianos were produced, employees built plane engines. The workers were women.

Job shortages during the Depression had caused most women to work at home. But with the war, women were building trucks and tanks and ships. Women were building fighter planes and teaching soldiers to fly them. "Rosie the Riveter" convinced the world that she could do anything.

Philip Wrigley believed she could even play professional ball.

• • • •

Wrigley acted quickly, believing that baseball's future depended on its survival during the war. Professional teams of young women, he decided, would be America's wartime athletes. Older women at work in the factories would be the audience. And after the war, Wrigley guessed, there would be twice as many fans flocking to his stadium.

He began work on his professional women's league during the winter of 1942, aided by advertiser Arthur Meyerhoff, lawyer Paul Harper, and Ann Harnett, who had organized women's softball teams in Chicago's playgrounds.

Wrigley's original plan was to professionalize women's softball. Amateur softball had been popular with American women for forty years. But semi-pro women, who competed against men and often beat them, were not well received by spectators. Dislike of female athletes lingered from the early part of the century, when women were expected to behave differently than men. Most American women had not even been allowed to vote until 1920; men, thought to be naturally strong and aggressive, were believed better suited to make stressful decisions, to appear and to argue in public. Even when Roosevelt promoted the building of public parks and athletics for all to boost Depression-era morale, old-fashioned ideas persisted. Most team sports came to have two sets of rules: one for stalwart males, another for less vigorous females. Softball was the same for men and women, however, because it was already a modification of "men's" baseball.

By 1942, when Wrigley was forming his professional women's league, the sight of a woman wearing pants was no longer shocking or offensive, as it had been when women began playing semi-pro softball. But women who competed too aggressively were still frowned upon.

"The fans don't particularly like women's softball, where a gal who looks like Joe hits it out of the park," Arthur Meyerhoff said. "If people want to see tomboys play softball, they'll go to the city park and watch for free. If they plan on paying for tickets, they'll want to see ladies and professionals."

Meyerhoff had another concern. If Wrigley wanted to keep people interested in baseball during the war, shouldn't the new girls' league play hardball instead of softball?

Wrigley agreed, but he worried that there would be few young women skilled enough to play pro-caliber baseball. There wasn't time to train athletes from scratch. Since softball was popular and available to women of all incomes, Wrigley's committee invented a hybrid of softball and baseball. Underhand pitches of a 12-inch ball and 65-foot basepaths were taken from softball, but runners were allowed to lead off and steal bases, as they did in baseball.

Overall, Wrigley's new nine-player game was similar to baseball in the 1800s.

The primary difference was that Wrigley's game would be a ladies' game. "We wanted a show of women, to take advantage of the charm of women," Meyerhoff said. "It was our feeling that if a girl walked up to bat as a girl—not a big bozo—and if she walked in the style of a model, that it would be much more spectacular if that gal hit that ball a way out than if an already strong character who was more masculine would do so." There would be, he said, both "spectacle" and "dramatic impact" in "seeing baseball, traditionally a men's game, played by feminine-type girls with masculine skill." Spectacle and drama were sure to sell tickets.

To heighten the element of surprise, Wrigley had a special dress designed for players to compete in. Short dresses worn with satin panties would make players look like All-American Girls—the name that was chosen for the new league.

Looks alone would not be enough: ballplayers had to be well-mannered both on the field and off. Wrigley did not want reporters to write, as they did of semi-pro softballers, that these female athletes hollered, cursed, and looked like men. In his League, Wrigley demanded that players behave and dress like ladies. They would always wear skirts in public. Their hair would be at least down to their collars. They would never smoke or drink in public. Their social engagements would be approved by team management.

Wrigley's All-American Girls would also play exhibition games for soldiers at training camps, and visit military hospitals. They would sell war bonds and teach young children how to play baseball.

Wrigley asked a lot of prospective players. In return, he offered a job opportunity that American women had never

*The All-American uniform—a compromise
between fashion and function.*

dreamed possible, and he promised to pay his players well. He invested $100,000 of his own money to start the All-American Girls League, with $22,500 going to each of four first-year teams. The $10,000 left over was to run the League's office in Chicago. Wrigley at first hoped to establish Girls League teams in cities that already had men's major-league teams, but this plan met with resistance from other team owners who believed that fans would not come to both men's and women's games. Travel restrictions sparked such fears. During World War II families were allowed just 3 gallons (11 liters) of gas a week for nonessential driving. In 1943, cars might travel only 40 miles (64 kilometers) on that amount.

So Wrigley began looking at smaller industrial cities near Chicago, places where war-industry workers needed entertainment. He looked for cities close enough together to let players bus to games. (The government allowed extra gas for people carpooling to work.)

South Bend, Indiana; Kenosha and Racine, Wisconsin; and Rockford, Illinois, were the first volunteers to host teams from the All-American Girls Professional Ball League. Local businesses matched Wrigley's contribution, giving each town $45,000 to establish a team. Investors felt sure that the teams would pay them back, not in money but in goodwill, for Wrigley had designed the League as a nonprofit organization. Any money left after paying player and management salaries would be given to host cities to build parks, playgrounds, gyms, or athletic programs.

Wrigley had the game, the places, and the money. All he needed now was players.

• • • •

Jimmy Hamilton knew how to find baseball players. After a lifetime in the game, scouting for the Chicago Cubs and managing minor leaguers, Hamilton had seen what small-town America had to offer.

Hamilton was the leader of thirty Cubs scouts who expanded their 1943 tours, drafting players for Wrigley's Cubs and Wrigley's new Girls League. Finding female athletes seemed impossible at first, for many schools in the 1940s didn't offer athletics for girls. Some doctors then believed that exercise would prevent girls from developing into child-bearing women.

Experienced scouts like Hamilton looked at high schools anyway. Outstanding female athletes sometimes played on boys' teams. Towns short on boys would complete squad rosters with girls. Mixed teams would be disqualified from playoffs, but that was a gamble small high schools had to take.

Village churches offered even better scouting grounds. Many churches owned gyms and encouraged girls to play on church-league softball and basketball teams.

If schools or churches had nothing to offer, girls often created their own teams. They chose an organized sport, enough friends for a team, and a coach, who scheduled meets and found a sponsor to purchase equipment. Local papers reported on these teams, giving scouts more talent to study and choose from.

Next stop: the Girls Athletic Association (GAA), an after-school club where girls learned soccer, volleyball, bowling, skating, swimming, golfing, and more. Hamilton even considered GAA coaches. Women piloting amateur teams were often just out of high school or college, young enough to fit Wrigley's definition of "girls," ages fifteen to twenty-five.

The girls next door to the United States were recruited, too, for Canada had a long tradition of organized women's sports. Canadian Bonnie Baker, a catcher visiting the

States in 1943 to compete in the World Softball Championship, was signed to an All-American contract, then sent home to enlist more Canadians. "Pretty Bonnie Baker" was a scout's dream and later a media darling, combining beauty and charm with prowess on the field.

Finally, Hamilton never left a town without exploring its industrial leagues. Roosevelt's "New Deal" had encouraged American businesses to promote recreational programs. Company bowling, basketball, and softball teams gave employees exercise, energy, and an incentive to work. Community residents liked rooting for their neighbors and applauded team sponsors. Industrial leagues were good business.

Baseball was an even better business, and parents were thrilled when Hamilton, scouting for the Cubs, asked their sons to try out for the team. Men's baseball was familiar; everyone knew a fellow could earn a living at it. But parents were not pleased when Hamilton considered their daughters for a professional team. No one had heard of Girls Professional Ball. No one had heard of professional women's sports teams. True, some women had become well known in tennis, swimming, skating, and golf. But only a few female athletes, such as 1932 Olympic track star Babe Didrickson, actually earned a primary income through sports competition and exhibition.

Furthermore, parents in 1942 thought their twenty-year-old daughters were too young to leave home. So scouts assured parents that every team would have a chaperone, just like sports teams at girls' colleges. The chaperone would be a woman of sound character who would look after the girls, approve social engagements, act as nurse, and make sure every player was in bed by curfew. Host cities would also look after the players. All-American Girls would live with trustworthy families, two players to every home. This would give girls an instant network of friends in their new communities.

Hamilton knew it would take more than talk to get the parents' approval. So, wearing his signature sports jacket, Hamilton took prospective players and their families to dinner. He surprised many people with his genial, soft-sell approach, never pressuring, always pleasant.

Years later, many Girls Leaguers would remember their dinner with Hamilton as the first they'd ever had in a restaurant. During the Depression, there was no money for such extravagance. The girls remembered not knowing how to order, which silver to use, what to do when a waitress brought a new plate. Hamilton probably understood, had probably seen the same response from dozens of boys he'd recruited. So Hamilton talked about how the game would let young folks see more of the country, and earn a good living, too.

How good? many fathers wanted to know. It depended on the girl, Hamilton told them—but forty-five dollars a week to start. Dad would look at Mother; Daughter would look at Dad. Everyone's eyes would widen. Forty-five dollars was often more than Dad earned in a week, and Jimmy Hamilton knew it. It was more than a man in Class D baseball, more than a girl working as a stenographer, more than a schoolteacher made in an entire month.

Why so much? was the next question. The Girls League would keep a tight summer schedule, Hamilton explained, playing a game every day, and sometimes two. Since players could not hold a second job, Wrigley made one job attractive.

What about player expenses on the road, hotels and eating out? Parents had heard of minor-league baseball men spending most of their earnings on such things. Hamilton promised that All-American Girls would have all expenses paid. Teams would travel together, lodge in nice hotels together, and eat together in restaurants that didn't serve liquor.

Hamilton could see when parents were weakening. Ever think about sending your girl to college? he might ask. Most parents would say yes, but they could never afford it. Girls League players could save their earnings, Hamilton pointed out, and pay for their own schooling. An athletic career doesn't last forever, but education does.

He saw longing in the eyes of the girls, worry in the eyes of the parents. He saw the same longing when he talked to young men about joining the Chicago Cubs: the look of young people wanting to test their wings, to escape the more predictable jobs they knew lay in wait. He saw parents who wanted their children's dreams to come true.

Hamilton ended these evenings by urging parents to just let their daughter audition. There would be four teams, he reminded them, with a fifteen-player limit per team. Only sixty girls would make it, but eighty would try out. Every girl would get a free trip to Chicago, her hotel, train fare, and meals paid for. It was a chance to see the city and a chance to experience how the League treated its ladies. Finally, he reminded them it was a chance to do something for the war effort: Profits would go to worthy local causes, and military personnel would be admitted free to all games.

If parents agreed to the tryout, Hamilton knew he had won the fight. He would then drive the family home, head to his hotel, and check in with Ken Sells in Chicago.

GROUND
RULES

Time was short: Girls League president Ken Sells had only four months to create four teams.

Following Wrigley's instructions, Sells began bombarding host cities with publicity weeks before the tryouts. Helped by the Wrigley Company staff, Arthur Meyerhoff's employees, and the Chicago Cubs organization, Sells sent host newspapers press releases about auditions, hometown hopefuls, and the upcoming game schedule. Reports of Wrigley's $100,000 contribution to the League and of "huge sums" from local businesses aroused local curiosity. So did League predictions that host cities would grow rich from tourism dollars. Meanwhile, the Kenosha paper offered a twenty-five-dollar war bond to the lucky winner of its "name the team" contest.

Sells discouraged local papers from writing their own articles, even about hometown girls, because Wrigley had firm ideas about his new League's image. Wrigley wanted to emphasize players' athletic skills along with more "feminine" talents such as cookie decorating. He wanted readers to believe that every All-American was "a symbol of health, glamour, physical perfection, vim, vigor, and a glowing personality." When there was no other news to print, the League kept itself in the public eye with "stories" about uniform colors.

Local interest peaked when four players, including League consultant Ann Harnett, were signed early so that they could tour League cities and encourage businesses to sponsor the new game. Newspaper writers, finally able to report their own observations, joked that these charming ambassadors would win ball games by batting their eyes at the umpires.

Meyerhoff reminded League officials that the game was most important. "You can put the most beautiful girl in the world on a baseball diamond," he warned, "but if she can't hit the ball, she's still a bum to the fans."

Sells listened. He signed three former major-league players—Bert Niehoff, Josh Billings, and Eddie Stumpf—to coach the girls. The Girls League would not be like the major leagues, Sells cautioned them. Niehoff, Billings, and Stumpf had worked for a system where every team chose its own talent and held its own spring training and its own tryouts. In the Girls League, all players would train and audition together. Coaches would create four equally matched teams, then draw straws to select teams. After the first year, teams would keep a core of established players, and new talent would be assigned on a team-need basis.

Men's baseball would wait nearly twenty-five years before creating a similar system, known as the free-agent draft.

Player contracts would also be unusual. As Wrigley told the press in February 1943, "Players have the option to renew from year to year at a definite predetermined and agreed-upon salary, which if not exercised by the League, leaves the player a completely free agent."

Major-league baseball would adopt this practice, too, but not until the 1970s.

Wrigley saw his Girls League as a chance to challenge management practices "which had been long established and volubly supported by both professional baseball leagues." He had seen pitfalls in the system, where a player became the "property" of the team who held his contract. Because the teams weren't equally matched, some suffered long losing streaks, frustrating their fans; others hid talent in the minor leagues, embittering young players who were kept from the majors.

Wrigley reasoned that teams of equal strength would be more exciting to watch, and more satisfying to play for. He later said, "I'm probably the only one in professional baseball in the last forty or more years who has never felt that the reserve clause as written in baseball contracts was really essential. I guess it is because I have sort of an old-fashioned idea that if a man likes his job he will give you his best. If he does not like it, no contract on earth can cause him to put forth his best efforts."

Yet there were aspects of the men's game that Wrigley wanted to preserve. During the life of the Girls League, nineteen major-league men would be hired to coach and pass along the secrets of the game. Wrigley even had plans for a women's minor-league system, expanding to cities like Chicago by 1944. In the meantime, Wrigley's Chicago ballpark was an ideal, centralized location for tryouts.

It was Sells's job to take care of the many details. He scheduled the girls' auditions around the Cubs' spring workouts at Wrigley Field. He hired coaches and umpires, arranging for coaches' off-season jobs and scheduling Girls League games around other local sporting events. Working with the established budget, Sells booked rooms at a plush hotel near the stadium, and estimated how much money would be spent there, at restaurants, and on transportation to get player hopefuls to Chicago and back home.

Expense records would help determine how much money would be needed for the next season. Long-range plans were important, for men's baseball could still be canceled if more men were needed for the war. And no one knew when the war would end. Although Americans had just entered the war, it had been going on overseas for years. No one could guess the fate of the world, let alone the fate of the game.

Three

LADIES' DAY

Most of the girls who were trying out arrived in Chicago by train. Many were still in high school, or had just graduated. They had grown up during the Depression, seldom crossing state lines, because most families didn't own cars. But trains, crowded with wartime travelers, were not frightening. Passengers gave their seats to soldiers, who insisted that ladies sit, instead. Strangers spoke with one another about scrap drives, blackouts, and war bonds.

America was different in 1943. Highway drivers, even women, were not afraid to give hitchhikers a lift. Doors to homes were seldom locked. Parents were not afraid to send their daughters to Chicago, and the girls were seldom afraid to leave home. After all, Ken Sells, the president of the entire League, took the time to meet unknown hopefuls as they got off the all-night train.

The greatest fear most girls had was that they would not be chosen for the League, that they would miss the chance "to get paid for doing something we would have done for free," as one, Irene Hickson, said. Irene wanted badly to make a team—she had dropped out of school so that she could work and play on her employer's teams. That had been the only way a woman could earn a living as an athlete until the Girls League came along. Irene had played every sport available and had even been promoted as a "girl boxer." She spent so much time competing that she wore her hair closely cropped and slicked back, like a boy's. Players like Irene confused Wrigley's scouts: She could play the game, but she wasn't exactly the "feminine type."

Wrigley hired Madame Helena Rubenstein, owner of the most famous charm school in Chicago, to teach deportment and grooming at spring training. Her task was to turn "tomboys" into "marygirls," her own description of attractive, appealing young ladies. Arthur Meyerhoff pointed out, "It's easier to teach a tomboy to act like a lady than to teach a lady to hit and run." Ken Sells reasoned that "a player is a performer. On stage or on the ball field, there is a responsibility to be attractive and to put on a good show."

The auditioning girls were taught to wear their hair in high bouffants, although baseball caps would never let them do so on the field. They learned to apply makeup, paint their nails, and select fashionable clothing. They studied the *Guide for All-American Girls* for tips on washing their faces, conversing with new people, and keeping fingernails clean by scratching a bar of soap before a game.

"I could see the point of them wanting us to be feminine," Irene would later say, "but I couldn't see the point of having to play that way. How could you wear all that makeup and your hair the way they wanted you to, and then go out there and play ball?"

Irene was not alone in her dislike of charm school. After a long day of catching, hitting, pitching, and running, with coaches evaluating every move and sending disqualified players home, the last thing anyone wanted to do at night was learn how to put on a coat or get out of a car gracefully.

"It's just a promotional deal," Irene reminded herself as she tottered across thick carpeting in high-heeled shoes, balancing books on her head. "This isn't so easy with a charley horse," another girl complained aloud, making it difficult for others to suppress their giggles under Madame Rubenstein's gaze. Others were glad that charm school taught them how to use all those forks in a restaurant. But it was added pressure for Irene, who had another fear: She was technically too old to be accepted into the League. Her twenty-eighth birthday was on its way, and Wrigley wanted players fifteen to twenty-five years old.

May 17–26, 1943, was a long week for auditioning players. No one wanted to answer a hotel telephone: It would probably be a coach with a message of dismissal. Girls who hadn't been cut tried to figure where the others had gone wrong: Had they failed on the field or at charm school? Nerves were taut. Some auditioning players asked for complimentary hotel cigarettes, retiring to their rooms, since the League forbade smoking in public. Older players were grateful to be allowed a beer with their dinner.

At last, it was May 26. The final cuts were made. The girls who saw their names posted screamed, jumped, hugged each other, and cried. Irene Hickson's name was there: She had agreed with League management to lie about her age. She joined the group of her future team-mates, leaving in a noisy pack to celebrate on the town.

It was a dream come true. But celebration was brief. Surviving spring training meant leaping straight into another grueling schedule. During the next three months, there would be 108 games, half at "home" and half away. All-Americans would play almost every day of the hot midwest summer, sometimes doubleheaders.

There were only four days left until the first game of the season, days that would be spent on the road playing exhibition games for soldiers in training. Players found those first games almost indescribable in later years: real games with winners, losers, and most important, an audience. They remembered soldiers teasing them for wearing pigtails. They remembered the crowd's sudden hush after a double play, followed by a surprised, approving buzz.

"I think they came to see our legs," some players said, "but they stayed because of the way we played." Short skirts were surprising in 1943. Although movie star Betty Grable was famous for bare legs, real-life women still wore hemlines past the knee. But other players pointed out that their thick wool knee socks were hardly "sexy," and neither was wearing spikes with a dress.

After exhibition games, players put on longer dresses and went to the on-base dance. "Sentimental Journey" was a popular song. The girls sang it, sometimes dancing with soldiers they might never see again, and sang it over and over on the dark, rattling bus to the next town.

HOME STANDS,
HOME FRONT

American women were surprised to discover how much they loved going to work. One wrote to the *Racine Journal-Times* in 1943:

Hurrying to catch an early morning bus: brown paper bags, thermos bottles of coffee and hot soup, "Baboushka-ed" permanents, lip-sticked smiles, bantering laughter, faded blue slacks, rolled up overalls, high-heels, grimy saddle shoes.

"Yeah, I made out pretty good yesterday! Whoever'd think I'd be sawing steel for airplane parts? I used to be a beauty operator! Some difference, eh?"

"I'm reading blueprints—tanks. Imagine me helping to assemble a tank! Why, I could never even follow a cake recipe and have it come out like the picture!"

"How's your housecleaning coming along, Sue?"

"Housecleaning? Don't you know I'm living with Mom again—for the duration? Yes, Jim wanted to enlist to help with the housecleaning overseas, mopping up the Axis, so I'm doing my bit here to help him make a clean sweep to Victory. What kind of work do I do? Sweeping, that's what!"

Ladies in overalls!

The letter was signed "Rose F. Rossa," and this was just the type of person Wrigley was looking for to offer a home to Girls League players. A person like Rose Rossa would know that Girls Baseball was good for morale, and a person like Rose Rossa would probably have an empty room at home because of a son's or husband's absence.

Wrigley wanted his ballplayers to live with families in the towns where they played, because young women in 1943 usually didn't leave home until they were married. By housing players with respected citizens, Wrigley would ensure their reputations as "nice girls." The community would get to know the players more quickly and be more eager to come root for the team.

Racine Belles business manager Thora Johnson recruited local families to house players. "We are not looking for anything fancy," she assured potential hosts, reminding them that their responsibilities would last only three months, and that they could charge a small room-and-board fee. As it turned out, many of the Girls Leaguers would come to think of their hosts as family, and stay with them year-round.

Johnson, like many Girls League advocates, saw beyond the business of baseball. She welcomed Racine's 1943 team sponsors by saying, "We believe there is a place for women in sports. We are, indeed, pioneers."

• • • •

All-Americans would have to earn their place in sports, but they found they already had a place in the hearts of their new cities.

Towns greeted their teams with luncheons, parties, and presentations. The *Racine Journal-Times* interviewed most Belles players before the team was one month old. Reporters followed Belles in town and out of town, writing about them like friends, using affectionate nicknames. Irene Hickson was dubbed "Choo-Choo," in honor of her Chattanooga birthplace (and the song "Chattanooga Choo-Choo"). Belles news topped the sports page, complete with season schedules.

The first games between the Belles and the nearby Kenosha Comets were full of "style, gay attire, and constant chatter," read the papers. The "chatter" may have been teeth: Players remember the midwest chill on bare legs and ball-swallowing fog from Lake Michigan. The "style" was in a game based on fundamentals and finesse. Sluggers like Kenosha's Ann Harnett and Audrey Wagner were rare. Most teams earned their runs one base at a time. Well-placed singles and bunts lured first basemen from their posts, forcing races to the bag. Walking, stealing, sacrifices—all were hallmarks of the All-American game. So was dedication, as teams didn't carry many backup players. Only a major injury took a player from the lineup. A pitcher starting a game would probably finish it.

That first-night Wisconsin audience rose to its feet and cheered. They came back, even though tickets cost seventy-five cents—more than fans would pay to see men's minor-league teams. Fan dedication was swift and steadfast: In 1943 a Kenosha crowd rushed the field when an umpire ruled against the Comets. In Racine, businesses closed during Belles games so that owners and customers could root for the girls.

The 1943 Racine Belles, with manager Johnny Gottselig and team mascot.

Racine's Edythe Perlick scoops one up for the camera.

Racine's Mary Nesbitt Crews takes a swing during warm-ups at Horlick Field.

Across the street from the ballpark, Racine's Bright Spot Cafe was decorated with photos of the Belles. The eatery opened after the last out, so that fans could buy players a soda or sandwich. Even during wartime sugar rationing, there never seemed to be a shortage of treats for deserving Belles.

The Belles loved playing at home. Not only did Racine's Horlick Field have the nicest showers and the cleanest locker room (thanks to a groundskeeper who "didn't put up with monkey business"), but its thick field was enclosed by a brick wall, like Wrigley Field in Chicago. Bands often played in the grandstand during games. Children would wait outside the locker room for player autographs before catching the city bus home. Players loved signing autographs at home. They had no all-night, out-of-town bus to catch. They could eat out with friends, go to bed if they were tired, even visit the other team's hotel.

It was against League rules for opposing players to "fraternize." But friendships had grown during spring training, and players knew, even if management didn't, that friendship could strengthen competition. All-Americans liked to compete against girls they knew, to win or lose against worthy opponents.

Home stands began with morning field practice. Afternoons could be spent resting, seeing friends, doing chores. At 5:00 P.M., it was off to the ballpark for batting practice, then the game. After that, showers and perhaps a bite to eat. Then the whole process began again. Of course, not all games would be completed. Because of civil defense air-raid rules, town curfews required darkness after a designated time. If games ran too long, they were suspended and completed on a later date.

Fans knew that players kept tough schedules, and so rewarded them with kindness: flowers or money for exceptional plays; chicken soup and cough drops for a catcher with a cold. This was true when the League was new, and years later, too. When Rockford's Ruth Richards broke her ankle on the last day of the season, fans collected six hundred dollars for her medical bills.

Sometimes, local families would adopt an entire team. The Berdinners of Racine never missed a home game and, every year, invited the Belles to a farm picnic. Each player's favorite food, as listed in the team yearbook, could be found at the Berdinner table: baked beans for Boston-born Madeline English, fried chicken for southern Anna May Hutchison. "We're going to the Berdinners'," Belles loved to joke, "and we're going to stay ber dinner."

Out-of-town players became celebrities, too. When they dropped in at the Bright Spot in Racine, fans asked for their autographs.

Mary Willmes, whose family owned the Spot, was in awe of baseball players. They must be so brave, she thought, so unlike herself. But once, a dark-haired girl from the bus smiled at Mary and asked if there were any mashed potatoes. This surprised Mary: Maybe ballplayers weren't so different after all. The next time Blackie Wegman's team came to town, Mary was ready with a steaming bowl of potatoes. It was the start of a friendship that lasted a lifetime. Blackie often wintered with the Willmeses after that.

Some All-Americans found off-season employment in the cities where they played. Being a Belle seemed all that Anna May "Hutch" Hutchison needed on her résumé at Western Publishing. After all, company owner Bill Wadewitz was also the Belles president. And if there was no work at Western Publishing, fans all over town asked their bosses to hire a Belle.

Belles star Clara Schillace,
who taught school in the
off seasons.

The Belles in a pregame rally huddle.

After work, players helped out in their adopted homes just as they would in their parents'. They washed dishes, stoked furnaces, cleaned windows and walls and clothes. "It wasn't as if I had a room and that's where I stayed," Hutch later remembered. There was a sense of freedom, a feeling of growing up. "My life's my own," Hutch declared. Hutch and her roommate moved in with the Days, whose son and daughter were overseas. When daughter Gladys Day returned, she and Hutch became such close friends that Hutch became a permanent member of the clan.

Adopted families, assigned at random, were sometimes as peculiar as real families.

Mary Carey and Alice DeCambra lived with two elderly sisters who enjoyed listening to Girls games on the radio. After much persuasion, the ladies finally attended a game at the park, and later told Carey and DeCambra what a nice time they'd had. They hadn't thought it fair, however, that the other team held onto "the stick" for so long and hit the ball all over the field, while the home team held it only a couple of minutes and didn't hit the ball at all.

• • • •

At the end of the 1943 season, Kenosha and Racine faced off for the first Girls League championship. Gate receipts would be used to send a girl from the winning host city to college.

The Scholarship Series was for best three out of five, and Racine had won the first two. In the third game, the score was tied 3–3 in the eighth inning when Belles catcher Irene Hickson doubled, then stole third. Second sacker Sophie Kurys walked and swiped second. Kenosha pitcher Helen Nicol countered by walking Racine slugger Edie Perlick, betting that the next Belles batter, Eleanor

Dapkus, would hit into a double play. It was a good gamble: Dapkus had not hit well in the series. But now she blistered Nicol's first pitch into left field, scoring both Hickson and "Sophie the Trophy." Dorothy Wind singled in Dapkus, bringing the score to 6–3, and Racine captured the first Girls League series.

Some players went home to their families when the winter months came; others found they felt at home in their adopted cities. But go or stay, win or lose, players spent winter waiting for summer. If home is where the heart is, the ballpark was home.

WINS AND LOSSES

It was a whole new ball game in 1944. The name of the game became official: Girls Baseball. Wrigley had originally baptized his league the All-American Girls Softball League. But he wanted no confusion between his league's brand of ball and traditional softball, which was now being played by a new professional women's circuit in Chicago. Wrigley franchised his game in 1944. Cities now purchased the right to play Girls Baseball.

A $25,000 franchise fee from each host city, plus three cents from each ticket sold, gave Wrigley funds to hold spring training, pay all salaries, buy liability insurance, print tickets, and advertise. He hired scouts and worked them hard to keep promising players away from Chicago's National Girls Baseball League (NGBL).

The two league names confused the public: the words "Girls Baseball" were common to both. But the National

Girls Baseball League played softball, plain and simple. The All-American Girls Baseball League mixed softball and baseball in a game that changed, over the years, into regulation hardball. There were other league differences: NGBL players wore slacks; All-Americans, skirts. The NGBL stayed in Chicago, while Wrigley's league started in four cities and grew.

Two All-American teams were added in 1944, the Minneapolis Millerettes and the Milwaukee Chicks. Wrigley sponsored these teams himself, with no local investors. He wanted Girls Baseball to expand to larger cities and share stadiums with men's minor-league baseball teams.

Unlike the first Girls League teams, the 1944 expansion squads struggled. Wrigley's sponsorship meant that local businesses had no monetary reason to promote Girls Baseball. And without community backing, the All-Americans were just one of many groups vying for big-city media coverage. Journalists in Milwaukee and Minneapolis often ignored pre-written stories from Wrigley's publicity machine, relying on their own observations. In July 1944, the *Milwaukee Journal* compared Girls Baseball with the local men's version played in the same stadium, and questioned the need for both. Milwaukee fans expressed displeasure at the seventy-five-cent Girls ticket price, when the established men's teams charged about the same.

Despite the unfavorable press, the Chicks won the 1944 Girls League championship. Yet they could not win the heart of the big city. The champion Chicks quit Milwaukee at the end of the season and relocated to Grand Rapids, Michigan, in 1945.

Meanwhile, in Minneapolis, news coverage went from bad to worse as the Millerettes lost game after game. The stadium was virtually empty every night. Visiting All-American teams usually paid for road trips with a share of the host park's gate; low gate receipts in Minnesota meant that the entire League lost money. By mid-season, the Millerettes left Minneapolis for good. They remained in the League as a traveling squad, the Minneapolis Orphans, playing every game on someone else's field, spending every night away from home.

Most of the Orphans relocated in 1945 to Fort Wayne, Indiana, where they became the Daisies, the winningest team in the League's history. Future Girls League All-Stars who started with the Orphans included slugger Elizabeth Mahon, rifle-armed catcher Ruth "Tex" Lessing, and 20-win pitcher Dottie Collins.

The fact that men's ball proved such strong competition for Girls expansion teams convinced Wrigley that the war would not stop major-league ball. He returned his attention to the Cubs and sold the Girls League to Arthur Meyerhoff. Meyerhoff believed his new investment was a sound one: Even with two failed franchises, 1944 attendance had improved forty-nine percent.

Change of ownership did not alter the makeup or momentum of Girls Baseball. In 1945, with six teams in supportive, midsized cities, the All-Americans prospered. At season's end, Connie "Iron Woman" Wisniewski became the first winner of the All-American Player of the Year award. Pitcher Wisniewski had moved with the Milwaukee franchise to Grand Rapids. There she built an astonishing earned run average (ERA) of 0.81, with a league-leading 32 victories.

Her title brought another victory to the Girls League: Wisniewski was pictured on the back cover of the 1946 *Whitman Guide to Major League Baseball*, a respected annual which that same year pictured major-league pitcher Hal Newhouser on the front. True enough, the publisher was Racine's Western Publishing, whose president also

Belles gathered for this publicity photo are, from left, Edythe Perlick, Doris Barr, Mary Nesbitt Crews, Janet Jacobs, Anna May Hutchison, and Irene Hickson. The 1943 championship trophy is on display.

The 1944 Belles plan their strategy before the fans arrive at Horlick Field.

owned the Belles. But picturing Girls Leaguers beside major leaguers was a departure from Wrigley's original soft-selling of women's athletics. Girls Baseball was aspiring to be more than a substitute for the men's game.

Such dreams would soon be tested. The most important victory of 1945 was announced during an August 15 doubleheader between the Racine Belles and the Fort Wayne Daisies. The game was interrupted by an urgent crackling of the public-address system: Japan had surrendered. The war was over.

Fort Wayne Daisy Faye Dancer turned cartwheels in the outfield until she couldn't see straight. Teammate Pepper Paire leaped into a nearby fountain, still in full uniform. For days, fans streamed to Horlick Field in record numbers to find a place and a means to celebrate. Single-game attendance broke records with a crowd of 4,077 on August 17, as the Belles battled for fourth place in the League.

Belles fan Beth Johnson would remember the end of the war both for its joy and its pain. Arriving early as usual at Horlick Field on August 15, Johnson found Irene Hickson alone in the dugout. Irene held a telegram that said her brother would not come home. Johnson thought of Irene every time the Belles took their pregame formation the remainder of that season. In a tradition that began with the League's first game, host players lined up between home plate and third base and visitors from home to first base, the two opponents joined in a "V" for "Victory." During the war, "The Star Spangled Banner" had played amid silent hopes for the war's end. After the war, the "Victory" formation brought cheers from tear-streaked faces.

All-Americans had wished and prayed for peace with the same fervor they had wished to play professional ball. Many players didn't consider that the end of the war could mean the end of Girls Baseball.

During World War II, the Racine Belles took exhibition tours to military training camps. The tradition continued after the war.

Wartime All-American games began with a "V for victory" formation.

The Belles were the first All-American team to take to the airwaves, promoting sales of war bonds and game tickets on radio.

Meyerhoff knew that, with the war's end, professional men's teams would soon be back to prewar standards. Gas rationing would be lifted, and fans could once again drive to the major leagues.

But Meyerhoff also knew that Girls Baseball had become more successful with each of its three seasons. In Racine and Fort Wayne, All-Americans had not only competed with local men's teams, but outdrawn them. He decided not to give up without a fight. Meyerhoff suspected that All-Americans had an advantage the competition couldn't overcome: They had become the girls next door. Their cities loved them, and advertiser Meyerhoff knew that love cannot be bought.

• • • •

The League continued to grow after the war, adding two successful expansion teams in 1946. The Muskegon Lassies gave Michigan its second Girls team in as many years. Illinois added the Peoria Redwings to its Rockford Peaches, for a total of eight teams.

The game itself changed, to keep pace with the advancing skills of veteran players. Both athletes and audience wanted to be challenged.

Anna May Hutchison had spent two years as a little-used catcher on the Racine bench, second to Irene Hickson. To keep busy, Hutch volunteered to throw pregame batting practices. She threw naturally, since it was only warm-up, with a "buggy-whip" sidearm delivery. If batters could hit her, she figured, they could hit the underhand offerings.

Coach Leo Murphy liked Hutch's style. He wanted her to pitch for real, but Girls Baseball rules had allowed only underhand pitches in 1945. "Murph" summoned new League president Max Carey, the former major leaguer

Grand Rapids Chick Viola "Tommie" Thompson shows the underhand pitch required by the League until 1946.

who had coached the 1944 champion Chicks. Carey enthusiastically proposed a change of rules to Meyerhoff; he had seen other Girls League pitchers lean toward the side-arm style.

By the end of 1946, Hutch was an All-Star, pitching 51 games for the Belles and winning 26 of them with a 1.62 ERA. That year, the mound-to-plate distance increased to 43 feet, accommodating the stronger pitchers. Basepaths grew to 72 feet, and the balls Hutch submarined were 11 inches around, one-half-inch smaller than the year before.

The new, smaller ball was popular with pitchers. Most batters hated it. But Rockford hurler Carolyn Morris disliked it, too. She had come to the League from a softball background and was used to large balls and underhand pitches. When the League stopped allowing underhand in 1947, Morris retired.

Hutch did not worry whether future pitching changes might force her from the game, too. Glad to be off the bench, she didn't complain when Murph used her in game after game. Hutch's arm couldn't possibly wear out. She was only twenty-one years old.

In the first 1946 playoff game against the South Bend Blue Sox, Hutch pitched seventeen full innings for the Belles. She pitched another complete game to propel the Belles to the finals against the Rockford Peaches, and started three of those six championship contests. Racine's clinching win was described by Hall of Famer Max Carey as "barring none, even in the majors, the best game I've ever seen." Fans were riveted for sixteen scoreless innings, with Racine fielders shielding themselves against thirteen Rockford hits. Racine scratched only three hits until the final inning when Sophie Kurys rapped a base hit, stole second, then rocketed home on a teammate's single.

Racine became the first All-American team to win the championship twice. This distinction added to Racine's status as the first team to organize under Wrigley, the first to win the championship, the first to obtain a team franchise, to publish a yearbook, to broadcast its games on the radio, to win the Opening Day Attendance Trophy, and to travel by chartered flight. The Belles' victory meant a sixty percent share of playoff gate receipts, to be used for public service and player bonuses.

• • • •

One month after the 1947 Brooklyn Dodgers left their training site in Havana, Cuba, America's "Béisbol Femininos" arrived. Choosing a foreign country for spring training proved to be one of the most ambitious Girls League publicity stunts ever.

The All-Americans landed in Cuba on April 21 on small flights from Miami, some carrying as few as eighteen people. More than two hundred players, managers, chaperones, administrators, and reporters would spend two weeks in the capital city, playing in the Gran Estadio de la Habana.

The Cuban press was even more attentive than League city papers back home. A full-page story heralded the League's arrival. Streets were lined with cheering fans. Police cars, with sirens blaring, escorted the girls to their hotel. Luckily, the hotel was across the street from the stadium, for every morning and every afternoon, a crush of bodies waited for the "Muchachas." Police would lock arms in two opposing lines, making a path for the All-Americans to dash through.

It was a giddily exciting time. Young women who had been thrilled to see Chicago were now being adored in a foreign land. Most Cubans didn't speak English. The food was exotically inedible; some All-Americans subsisted on fruit and milk. Braver girls sampled alligator steaks.

Twice, plans to visit the capitol building were foiled by political unrest. On Cuba's Labor Day, May 5, All-Americans were confined in their rooms as Havana's streets were flooded with demonstrating citizens. Businesses closed, although street vendors were in good supply. Resourceful All-Americans lowered baskets of money from their hotel balconies and asked obliging young Cuban men to fetch fruit and soda.

On the following day, the city returned to normal. Shops opened. Returning All-Americans and prospective rookies trained on the field from 10:00 A.M. until 1:00 P.M. Afternoons were filled with "chalk talks," discussions of strategy, and managerial meetings to speed up player allocations.

By the first weekend, teams were assembled. A round-robin tournament began; batting practice brought rows of spectators, cheering each All-American move. When the first pitch flew, 15,000 Cubans were there to see it. In all, 50,000 people came to cheer the "Americanas." The numbers would have been higher if the stadiums had been bigger. All-Americans were honored that, in baseball-mad Cuba, they had attracted more fans than the great Brooklyn Dodgers.

The Racine Belles returned with a surprising souvenir. Her name was Eulalia Gonzalez, or "Viyalla" (the smart one). Like many All-American players, Viyalla had grown up playing with and against men's teams, and had quickly adapted to the American game. Although she lacked both a second language and a birth certificate, she was given special permission by Cuban President Ramon Grau to

Batting practice at the stadium in Havana, Cuba.

Political unrest prevented All-Americans from leaving their Havana hotel rooms, but Cubans on the street below fetched sodas for the "Béisbol Femininos."

leave her country. Homesickness took Viyalla back to Cuba before the season was out, but other Cuban women would later join the League as a result of the 1947 training tour.

• • • •

The Belles returned to Racine like the conquering heroines they were. As the winners of spring training's Esther Williams Trophy, they were pictured at the top of Racine's front page, waving from a chartered bus window like a politician on a whistle-stop tour. At their first home game of 1947, the Belles raised the 1946 championship flag over Horlick Field. The mayor threw out the first pitch.

Such success, at home and abroad, led Arthur Meyerhoff to dream of League expansion to Florida, California, Cuba, and South America. A MovieTone news release, filmed in Cuba, raised national awareness of the midwestern Girls League. The newsreel appeared in American movie theaters one year after it was filmed. By then, it was out of date.

In 1948 overhand pitching replaced sidearm, and the Girls League pitching distance increased by 7 feet. Balls, diminished from 11 inches to 10⅜, now traveled 50 feet from mound to home plate. Basepaths remained at 72 feet.

Perhaps the most popular game change would take place in 1949, when the ball shrank to 10 inches. Red seams convinced fans that this was a regulation baseball, even though it was actually an inch too large; without red seams, the same 10-inch ball brought complaints from fans that the players were using a softball. At mid-season the smaller ball demanded a further extension of the pitching distance, this time to 55 feet. "Just three-eighths of an inch and red seams has made more friends for the game than you can imagine," a scout would write to Meyerhoff.

Even Racine coach Norm Derringer said, "The only difference I could see between Girls Baseball and men's was the distances. They both could hit and run, bunt and steal, fake bunt and steal. When a game was on, they played to win. And they played hurt to protect their salaries." Derringer felt that the new ball size was a step in the right direction. "Players could do a lot more with the same kind of ball as the major leagues use," he said.

A regulation 9-inch baseball would not be adopted until 1954. By then, basepaths were near regulation at 85 feet, and pitching only a half-foot short of the major-league 60 feet. Contrary to expectations, many Girls League batting averages soared when the regulation ball was used. Kalamazoo Lassie June Peppas, whose best batting average (BA) in six seasons had been .285 in 1951, notched an impressive .333 in 1954.

Not every change was popular. In the late 1940s, Meyerhoff called a meeting to introduce new caps, visors that would allow players to wear their hair teased stylishly high during games. He also presented heavier makeup requirements.

His plans were met with dismayed silence. Then one player stood. "How are we supposed to keep our hair neat and in place with a cap like that?" she demanded. "And how are we supposed to wear mascara and lipstick in 90-degree weather and not have it melt and smear?"

The silent room exploded with voices. The new caps never made it to the playing field.

Meanwhile, the League's 1948 overhand pitch, a blessing to some pitchers, was a blow to others. Racine's Hutch could throw overhand, but just throwing at all seemed to be getting more and more difficult. After 26 wins in 1946 and 27 the following year, Hutch had won only 3 out of 14 in 1948. Her ERA zoomed from 1.38 to 3.67, and she walked a batter almost every other inning. Hutch didn't know what was wrong, but some of the coaches knew. They'd seen this happen in the major leagues when a young pitcher had a terrific first season. The team needed good pitchers to win. But a pitcher's arm needed rest to last.

After two years of pitching 300 innings, Hutch's arm had worn out. She was traded to Muskegon.

Hutch had been with the Belles for five years. She knew the town. She knew the people. She was more homesick leaving Racine than she'd been leaving her own parents in Louisville, Kentucky. Her statistics improved a bit in Muskegon; her win-loss record shrank to 8–12. The fans were nice, her new teammates, too—but it just wasn't the same. Hutch retired at the end of the 1949 season. She was twenty-four years old.

ON THE
ROAD

Grand Rapids to Springfield was a nine-hour drive. Some people could sleep on the bus, though they'd wake up occasionally to complain, "I think these towns do road construction at night just to keep us awake."

Players who couldn't sleep on a bus bouncing from one League town to another crowded the aisles, shooting craps and playing poker. Card games could be short-lived if the deck was blown out the window, or pitched out by an unhappy gambler. Sometimes, a single voice began to sing, "She'll be comin' 'round the mountain when she comes. . . ." By the end of a mile, most of the passengers joined in, along with a harmonica and a ukelele, too.

Belle Anna May Hutchison remembered another popular way to pass time on the road during her playing days.

"I've really got to *go!*" she'd tell Coach Murphy again and again, till he finally sighed and told the bus driver to pull over. Hutch and two other Belles would hop off and run together into the roadside weeds. They knew Murph's heavy gray sweats, worn for luck, were damp and itchy. He was anxious to get to the hotel and out of them. The girls took their time.

"I hope you get poison ivy!" he shouted into the darkness. The girls on the bus laughed out loud.

• • • •

The sight of city limits meant action on Girls League buses. Players hunted for skirts to pull on over their shorts. Mirrors, combs, and lipstick made the rounds, especially when the girls were visitors arriving mid-morning.

Hotel check-in time wasn't until noon. Early arrivals would browse about town, eat breakfast at a diner, window shop, pause at the library. After check-in, All-Americans could shower and sleep until 5:00 P.M., when it was time to go to the park. Traveling teams didn't take practice until just before the game.

The morning after the game, some visiting players attended church. Others waited until the afternoon to go out, catching a movie matinee for a quarter.

Some stayed at the hotel and mended their road clothes. Since uniforms had to be dry-cleaned, which was difficult on the road, players made two suits last an entire trip. If a uniform couldn't be mended, the player would inherit another—along with its new number. Roommates changed frequently, because chaperones wanted everyone to become friends. Belles Irene Hickson and Eleanor Dapkus were seldom separated, however, because both loved to sleep past noon.

Players made the most of their time off between games, especially on doubleheader days. Doubleheaders meant double duty for everyone except pitchers. The first game was nine innings, the second was seven. In case of a tied score, either game could be longer.

South Bend was an unpopular site for doubleheaders. Players said the rocky infield was asphalt or, as they privately called it, "ass-felt."

If a game was particularly rough, the team manager might buy everyone a meal. The road trip instantly turned into something special. The whole team didn't often get together just for fun—unless bus rides counted as fun. All-Americans who had joined during the first three years thought that bus rides were special. They remembered riding crowded wartime trains that were sometimes so late that players had to jump off and jog to the ballpark.

Disabled players were not supposed to travel; they were supposed to stay home and rest. But injured athletes often miss the action, even feel worse without it. When Rockford's Jackie Kelley Savage had a dislocated shoulder and teammate Alice Pollitt Deshaine had one leg in a cast, they drove, like a team, to an out-of-town game. Jackie steered with her good hand and worked the pedals. "Al" did all the shifting.

• • • •

A chaperone's job was to discourage such impetuous behavior, seldom an easy task: "Chappies" were often not much older than the girls. Some had played Girls Baseball and understood all too well the high spirits, the camaraderie, the way makeup and tempers could melt in the sun.

Maintaining decorum was only part of the job. Chaperone Mildred "Willie" Wilson of the Racine Belles bandaged slider Sophie Kurys before and after every game. She gave pitcher Joanne Winter a rubdown and massage. She accompanied players to the doctor to make sure orders were followed. Herself a former athlete, she cheered from

In 1946, the Racine Belles became the first All-American team to travel by air, flying to engagements across Lake Michigan.

Grand Rapids manager John Rawlings helps carry equipment to the stadium.

Chaperone Mildred "Willie" Wilson administers first aid to Joyce Hill Westerman, who appears to be laughing but is actually grimacing with pain.

Mickey Maguire and Whitey Whiting take a break at Grand Rapids in 1945.

the bench or gave advice during games, or ran right onto Horlick Field to administer first aid.

A chappie told players of business appointments, luncheons, and speaking engagements. She helped players learn how to speak in public.

A chaperone herded the team out of the stadium or hotel and onto the team bus. She reserved the right number of hotel rooms for each road trip and gave players meal money, paychecks, and clean, mended uniforms. She gave the bus driver his orders, so he'd be in the right place at the right time.

Like players, chappies had diverse backgrounds. The Peaches' Dottie Green and others were former All-Americans. Like players, chappies often wintered in their League host cities. Willie Wilson and pitcher Joanne Winter even opened a candy shop together in Racine. During the season, though, players didn't see much of chaperones except on the field or on the bus.

Chaperones wanted to befriend players, but many girls were independent and didn't like to ask for help. Kenosha catcher Joyce Hill Westerman recalls sitting with her chaperone in dugouts and on the bus, talking about lots of things, but never about problems. "You kept problems to yourself," Westerman said, "and solved them yourself."

But then she seemed to be "crying a lot." Travel and tangled nerves had given her anemia. "My chaperone was so nice. She talked to me and said, 'Let's fix this.' I'd been overdoing to prove that I could do the job."

Chaperones had to prove themselves, too, but in different ways. Players wanted to know if chappies knew what was important, or if they would "fink to the coach" over trifles. So new chaperones were put to the test with pranks—snakes in their beds, toothpaste in Oreo cookies, short-sheetings, and Limburger cheese spread on hotel-room light bulbs.

After passing her trial, Racine chappie Willie Wilson became a partner in crime. One night, she brought cream puffs to the team hotel. Word went out among the Belles, "Go to Willie's. There's stuff to eat." The result was a food fight that would later be known as the Great Cream Puff Battle.

Appropriately, pitcher Joanne Winter led the attack against Willie, before being beaten back to the hall. The noise brought Coach Murphy. But by the time he had arrived, the girls' doors had shut and, suddenly, all was quiet. Murph followed a mysterious trail of white to Joanne's room and knocked on the door. Joanne answered with an innocent expression and smears of frosting on her face. "What cream puffs?" she said.

Murph shook his head, tried to hide a grin, and paid the hotel bill out of his own pocket. His players were on the honor system, and were expected to know what was fun and what was going too far. One food fight, he would let go. They wouldn't have another.

Other pranks became traditions. Racine rookies, and soon rookies from other teams, were baptized in the Racine cemetery. Driven to the graveyard after dark, newcomers were told to walk in front of the car's headlights. As the slow-moving auto approached a certain tall tombstone, an eerie play of light made it look as if the stone were rising in the air.

"If a rookie can run faster than the car when we peel out of there in second gear," laughed teammates, "you know she'll have a good, long career!"

Cemeteries were also where tired players unwound after games. After putting in an appearance for the chaperone's bed check, two or three girls would later sneak down the fire escape, then go to the dark graveyard to drink beer, tell stories, and talk to the headstones.

Even curfew didn't guarantee an end to mischief. League president Ken Sells once received a telephone call at four o'clock in the morning from singing All-Americans.

Players had fun on the field, too, within the limits of the game.

Grand Rapids coach John Rawlings had spent a lot of time teaching his team how to fake bunt and half-hit. When Alma "Ziggy" Zeigler hit too hard during a game, Rawlings pretended to faint.

Fans watched for the "Peppas wiggle" as Fort Wayne's June Peppas wriggled into batting position. They listened for Hutch's raucous, encouraging whistle, and laughed at the lighted bow tie she wore when she coached at third base. Faye Dancer, a Fort Wayne Daisy, was popular wherever she played. She often turned cartwheels on her way to the outfield. She spent time-outs catching fireflies and pinning them to her cap. She led bleacher cheers, ran warm-up laps backward, rubbed her bat "with potion to make it strong."

Dancer even had boyfriends in a number of towns. Once, she and teammate Pepper Paire found two boyfriends each had come to one game. The girls hid under the bleachers until the crowd—and the coast—was clear.

PLAY
BALL!

When Rockford pitcher Olive
Little was honored by fans with a pregame ceremony, she
credited teammates for her success. "We care for each
other," she explained.

What was true in Rockford was also true in Racine,
where rookie Anastasia Batikis learned base running from
superstar Sophie Kurys. Even though newcomers hoped to
replace older players in the lineups—maybe even because
of it—everyone believed in teamwork. Teamwork had
seen the nation through the Depression and the war. Teamwork was a way of life to All-Americans living with one
family in the summer, another in the winter, and a family
of teammates between times.

Nancy "Hank" Warren was struggling through her first
game as a Muskegon pitcher when catcher Dorothy
"Mickey" Maguire stalked to the mound and growled,
"Damn it, if you can't throw the ball to me, then throw it at
me!"

Rookies learned by listening and by watching. Mickey's young teammates once saw her catch both games of a doubleheader before coming to bat in the top of the ninth. With two out and a runner on, her team was down by one. Mickey drew a full count—three balls, two strikes—before hitting a line drive. She rounded first, then second, and on her way to third—fell. She got up, passed third, and fell again. The ball was coming in. She was about to be tagged. Her teammates were screaming. Mickey crawled, as fast as she could, touching home plate just before the tag. She caught the last half of the inning before going to the hospital for a badly bruised thumb, an injury that had taken place during the first game.

Rookies saw how a player prone to pregame jitters, like Kenosha's Joyce Hill Westerman, would get pep talks from teammates, coaches, and chaperones on the bus, in the locker room, on the field. "Come on, Joyce, I know you can do it!" Rookies soon joined the chorus of encouragement. And if opposing teams, folks in the crowd, or umpires let out a discouraging word, rookies and veterans alike were out to fight. Baseball has its occasional brawls, and the "Ladies League" was no exception.

Fort Wayne Daisy Pepper Paire was positive she was safe when she was called out on a slide. Leaping to her feet, she whirled to argue with the umpire and caught him on the jaw—with her fist. She stared down at him, hardly believing what had happened. "I suppose," he asked quietly from the dirt, "you know this means I gotta throw you out of the game?" The umpire was Lou Rymkus, a future Cleveland Browns tackle.

Grand Rapids Chick Ruth "Tex" Lessing hit an umpire on purpose. He got a black eye; Tex got a hundred dollar fine. To pay the bill, fans passed the hat, and raised two thousand dollars.

Pat Keagle of the Chicks had to be careful arguing with

umpires like Rymkus. He was tall enough to leave 5-foot-2-inch Keagle yelling right into his stomach. The fans loved it.

Some players were too shy or too polite to "mix it up." The Belles' Maddy English, on the other hand, upbraided an umpire in her native New England accent. She wasn't thrown out of the game, or even fined, because the umpire wasn't sure what she meant when she called him a "bahstahd."

Racine reporter Don Black satirized the umpire/player relationship in the 1946 Racine Belles yearbook when he wrote, "The umpire reprimanded Clara Schillace by saying: 'Youse are no lady,' and she retorted at him: 'Neither are you.' . . . She won that argument by a large margin."

Chaperones frowned on such behavior. Managers laughed. Even League president Max Carey shared stories of past shenanigans as a Brooklyn Dodgers outfielder. Veterans knew that a little mischief might rejuvenate players who had played a hundred games in as many nights. Athletes were tired, hot, and sore even before spending hours on rattling buses.

The game itself was hazardous. A bad-hop grounder could break a fielder's finger. The summer sun scorched bare arms and legs. A wild pitch could rip a batter's ear. Sliding into base meant gashes and bumps, as bare-armed infielders tagged spikes-first opponents. Some collisions broke bones. And even a good slide was no picnic in a skirt. "Strawberries," scrapes from sliding on bare skin, were common. Some girls claimed that sliding high on their rears solved the problem. Sophie Kurys, the League's champion base stealer, just bandaged her thighs every day. Strawberries were part of the game. Sophie's chaperone invented a raised sort of "doughnut" to put around the wounds, so that clothing wouldn't stick.

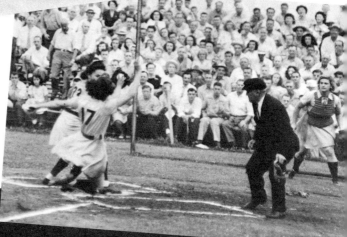

*Kenosha Comet
Helen Filarski tags
Peoria Redwing
Josephine Kabick.*

*Redwing pitcher
Josephine Kabick
goes for the tag
while covering
home for catcher
Joyce Hill West-
erman.*

*Playing under lights in 1946, Hutch (number 13) bunts in
a teammate while the opponents scramble for the out.*

Coaches encouraged hard play. Long-time Peaches coach Bill Allington supposedly told batters to "get a hit or get hit." Either way, the team got a base. And Allington wasn't surprised when the Peaches got a lot of bases. "Just show 'em the right right way to field or hit," he said, "and that's the only way they'll play for you."

Former Chicago Cub Woody English agreed. After coaching the Grand Rapids Chicks, he said, "They were talented, loyal, and had the right kind of team spirit. They looked up to me and would do anything on the diamond that I asked."

At Fort Wayne, with Chick Betty Wallens on first, English walked to the stands and asked front-row fans, "Do you want to see her steal second?" They did. He signaled. She did. "Do you want to see her steal third?" She did. English remembered years later what happened next. "Then those fans started ragging on me, saying 'You're afraid to have her steal home,' and I said 'You're damn right!' "

Coaches, like players, learned on the job. Bill Allington's Peaches once led the Daisies 20–0 in the ninth. Confident of a win, Allington sent all of the regulars to the showers and let the rookies play. In the last half inning, with the Peaches trying desperately to get three outs, the Daisies scored 21 runs and won the game.

Coach Norm Derringer of the 1950 Racine Belles would have done the same as Allington. He once told a columnist, "We could have won . . . if I had used veteran players in some of the tight spots. But we've got a good bunch of rookies, and the only way to develop rookies is to play them.

"These new girls are green and kinda scared when you first put them in ball games. Playing will give them confidence and experience. So you lose a few ball games. Well, losing them (early in the season) doesn't mean too much. You don't get anything special for winning them now, either."

Winning was important in the All-American League. But even an irreverent major-league veteran like Woody English held strong memories of what was most important in Girls Baseball.

"They were my friends," he said.

MINORS

When the Muskegon Lassies
yearbook printed a young girl's wish to "be a Lassie when
I grow up," other team sponsors wondered: Why wait till
she's grown?

If girls started playing ball sooner, there would be more
and better pros to recruit later. Junior teams would be a
perfect community service project for the nonprofit All-
Americans and other organizations that wanted to "fight
juvenile delinquency," a growing concern in the late
1940s. Interest and need were demonstrated when
Kiwanis-sponsored "Knothole Gangs" yielded hundreds
of children signing up to attend free home games.

The first All-American "juniors" team, the South Bend
Bobbie Soxers, appeared in 1946. Racine, Kenosha,
Rockford, Fort Wayne, and Muskegon followed soon af-
ter, calling their teams simply Juniors. In 1947, Racine's

four new Junior Belles teams were named for the colors of their uniforms. The Reds, the Grays, the Golds, and the Greens wore suits stylistically identical to the "Big Belles." A local store donated the fabric. Racine women sewed. Players would bring their own shoes and gloves, with the Big Belles donating equipment and umpire fees.

More than a hundred girls came to a Racine park for preliminary training sessions. Auditions would be two weeks later, after coaches knew the kids, how quickly they learned, and how hard they were willing to try.

"Some of them were so uncoordinated at first, they couldn't break a pane of glass," Junior Belles coach Herb Hoppe said of those early days. He'd played on semi-professional teams all of his life, and he liked these little girls who "wanted to practice every day."

Janet Wells was such a girl. Yet she scarcely believed it when her strict father read to her from the paper about Junior Belles training. "Papa, may I really?" she asked. He said, "Playing ball is good for you, go."

"We played like little toughies," Janet remembered. But after every inning, she would take out a comb and straighten her long, black curls.

The coaches assigned fifteen girls to each team. The youngest player was twelve; the oldest, fourteen. After players were assigned, coaches drew straws for groups, just as senior circuit coaches did.

After the formal, first-year auditions, hopeful Juniors players would visit a friend's team to try out. Coaches would watch prospects a few days before deciding. Teams couldn't carry too many youngsters, because every Junior played in every game.

It was hard for Hoppe to turn anyone away. He had kids of his own and knew there weren't many other activities for them in 1947 Racine. No wonder they wanted to practice every day. No wonder no one ever missed a practice or a game. Hoppe came home from work each day to find a neighbor's daughter in the drive, waiting to play catch. "We compromised and practiced three or four times a week," he said. Neither coaches nor players were paid for their efforts. Only umpires were paid, for the competitions that took place on Saturdays and Tuesdays.

Janet Wells said, "It was the honor of my life to be chosen." Her family understood. When a big wedding came up on the day of a game, Janet was taken to both. "There I am in the old pictures. Everyone is in gowns, and I'm in my pantalettes and little short dress. Everybody kept saying how cute my uniform was."

For girls like Janet, dedication paid off. "I took a lot of time with them," Hoppe said, "and after a while, they became good players. They learned to run and catch and slide. They learned to throw overhand, even curves." If someone told Janet she "threw like a boy," she considered it a compliment.

"They played hard," Hoppe said. "There was no fooling around."

Juniors games were held in city parks, with all four teams competing at once. Families like Janet's would walk from one game to the other, because Janet and her sister were on different Juniors teams. Employees of Big Belles sponsors often attended games to see friends, and to please their bosses. Hoppe himself worked for Western Publishing, a Belles benefactor. Almost everyone he knew from work came to Juniors games.

Juniors' umpires were local, a nice position for officials: If parents objected to a call, they did so politely, not wanting to insult a person they knew.

Herb Hoppe and his Junior Belles team, the Grays. Batgirl Linda Lou Hoppe is seated front and center.

What Juniors players loved best was playing at Horlick Field just before a real Belles game. "That was like being in heaven," Janet said. Afterward, Juniors attended the grown-up games for free, as they did any time they wore their caps to the ballpark. On very special occasions, Juniors teams traveled with the seniors. In 1952 the Junior Daisies and South Bend Bobbie Soxers took the field in Fort Wayne prior to a game by their "big sisters." But most Juniors competitions were between intra-city teams.

Local newspapers took Junior league baseball as seriously as adult play. Juniors tryouts, team rosters, and even uniforms were reported with the same enthusiasm given the older girls.

Hoppe could ask his employer for anything his team needed, even to miss an hour from work if he had to take care of baseball business. Employers were glad to have workers contribute to the community, and gave people like Hoppe the freedom to do so. "Times were different," Hoppe would say years later. "There wasn't as much stress. There was no one telling me to do this or that with my team. And I got to know some of the girls, some of the parents. You could feel you were doing something. You could feel the kids appreciated it."

Times were different in many ways. In 1947, fourteen-year-old girls were considered far too young to have boyfriends. They did have friends who were boys, and Hoppe remembered that boys often came to Juniors games, throwing warm-ups with the players they knew.

"One boy came to every game and hid behind a tree," Janet remembered. "He'd always ask me if I wanted to get a soda, and I always told him no."

Between work and Junior Belles ball, Hoppe said he "never had a day to myself." He made his eight-year-old daughter a batgirl so he could see her more often, and hoped that she would someday be a Junior Belle. But by 1950 the Belles, like other All-American teams, were beginning to struggle. The stress-free times Hoppe spoke of were rapidly disappearing, and Girls Baseball was a product of those times.

FORCE OUT

Even Arthur Meyerhoff could make mistakes. Attendance had improved so much between 1944 and 1948 that the League's board of directors, representing each team, decided to try big cities again. But expanding the 1948 Girls circuit with the Springfield Sallies and the Chicago Colleens was a repeat of the 1944 team failures in Minneapolis and Milwaukee. Both teams failed by the end of the season.

Perhaps Meyerhoff's biggest mistake was his honesty. He hoped to make money with Girls Baseball, and so he stopped calling the managing office a nonprofit organization. By the time Meyerhoff's League management paid for scouting, spring training, exhibition tours, and salaries, however, there wasn't much profit left over. Even so, local sponsors who were classified as involved with "not-for-profit" teams began to resent losing money when they thought Meyerhoff was making it.

Meanwhile, the cost of maintaining a team was growing. Seasoned players like Irene Hickson, who joined the League in its first year, became more valuable as qualified rookies became scarce in the late 1940s. Hundreds of girls auditioned every spring, but most came from softball backgrounds that didn't prepare them for stealing bases and hitting overhand pitches. Meanwhile, veterans throughout the Girls League grew anxious to attend college, marry, have children. To make sure talented players came back each season, local business sponsors offered cash bonuses on top of regular salaries. If more than one business wooed the same player, her signing bonus might add up to two or three thousand dollars. Patron "bonuses" made it worth a player's while to stay and play.

Under Meyerhoff, as with Wrigley, teams paid money to the League office based on gate receipts. Teams that made money shared with those that didn't. Racine, one of the most successful of the original four franchises, had helped to support other teams as they grew. After all, Racine needed competitors to have a ball game. It was reasonable to support their development, just as it was reasonable to have a nonprofit team. Projects such as public park development, paid for by the Belles, benefited the community and made the sponsoring businesses popular.

But sponsors like Bill Wadewitz, who had sustained the Racine Belles from 1943 to 1950, became upset when more and more money went to support teams that couldn't pay a fair share. This meant fewer dollars were available to spend on advertising. Without advertising, fans didn't come to the games. With no audience paying for tickets, there were no proceeds to spend on public projects like the Junior Girls teams. Without community goodwill, why have a team at all?

Belles attendance was 102,413 in 1946. The first dip

came in 1948, when 79,994 fans turned out. Racine, like other successful franchises, felt the burden of the new teams in Springfield and Chicago. League management tried to help by lessening franchise fees, but this resulted in less money to spend on publicity. The Belles cut back on some of their popular publicity features, such as live bands and radio broadcasts. In 1949, Belles fans numbered 44,912, and in 1950 only 29,000. Total League attendance went from a high of 910,747 in 1948 to 585,813 after the 1949 publicity budget cuts.

Even in 1950, when League attendance was at its lowest, fans like Racine's Beth Johnson never missed a game. A Grand Rapids watcher wrote a poem praising the Chicks for the local paper. Kenosha Comet Teeny Petras had to rescue an umpire from an angry crowd after he threw her out of a game.

In 1951 the Belles left Racine and moved to Battle Creek, Michigan. Some of the team's top stars—Sophie Kurys, Maddy English, Edie Perlick, and Joanne Winter—went together to Chicago to play in the National Girls Baseball League. The All-American League seemed too unstable.

The Muskegon team moved to Kalamazoo, Michigan, and both Rockford and Peoria were in financial straits before the end of the 1950 season. A Peaches fan club of 2,500 members raised $12,000 to keep the team in Rockford through the year. In Grand Rapids the fans couldn't raise enough, so Chicks players and coaches went on for no pay in a donated field. Then the team suffered a fire and lost all its uniforms. Peoria had folded by then, and the Chicks carried on in cast-off Redwing uniforms; there wasn't enough money for new. But most players still believed that playing ball, no matter what the circumstances, was better than not playing ball.

Local sponsors began pushing Meyerhoff for change. A 1949 decision canceled centralized spring training. Next, sponsors needing more local money voted to pay the League office one-and-a-half cents for each ticket sold, only half as much as before. The main office then lacked funds to take tour teams on the road for "seasoning," or playing experience. There was even less left over to spend on publicity.

In 1951, Meyerhoff gave in and sold the All-American teams to local owners. Advertising budgets continued to shrink. Attendance shrank, too. Without League rules to equalize teams, the Fort Wayne Daisies dominated. Each team did its own scouting now, but competition from the Chicago league was keen. The Chicago league tempted All-Americans, whose salaries were now frozen at a hundred dollars a week or less. Almost thirty dollars of that was to be spent on food.

Catcher Joyce Hill Westerman said, "Sometimes our checks were late, and that worried us. I guess they didn't have enough money." Players were doubling as chaperones and third-base coaches. Coaches like Norman "Nummy" Derringer started driving the team bus, with the promise of a little extra pay at the end of the season.

Derringer had started coaching in Racine in its final years. "We had an excellent backer in Racine," he said. "It was nothing for me to spend ten thousand dollars on a road trip. [Belles owner] Wadewitz just paid the bills. There was no kibbitzing." Derringer noted that a hotel bill for twenty to thirty team personnel could total between six and seven hundred dollars, no small sum in 1950.

Derringer saw the All-American League change from the "spend money to make money" philosophy of 1950 to "no backing at all in 1953 and '54."

Even the quality of ballparks began to suffer. Places like

Racine's Horlick Field were costly; during Meyerhoff's tenure, the Belles and other franchises had been responsible for paying rent, concessionaires, and business managers. Derringer's later, locally owned teams played "on football fields with no lights. I'd help the groundskeepers get the diamond ready myself."

This task was in addition to driving the bus after a hard game. "I'd be so sleepy. The girls would stand by me all night and talk and play cards to keep me awake.

"The camaraderie was just beautiful," he said. "It was one of the highlights of my life. It's too bad it had to end."

The end began in 1951, when the Belles moved to Battle Creek. The team never really got established in its new town; the Belles folded in 1952.

In Kenosha the Comets' season started on shaky ground: 1,200 fans came to the opening night game, and just 237 the next night. The local paper gave the team excellent coverage during the first half of the season, but as it became more and more obvious that there was no audience for the Comets, the paper ceased rooting for them and printed short, dry accounts of the Comets' final games. Only 568 fans showed up for the Comets' last out. Like the Belles, the Comets faded without fanfare. The last article the paper carried was of a road game. Kenosha lost.

By the end of 1954 just four teams were left in the circuit. They had taken to traveling in station wagons to save bus money. The final game of the final championship was forfeited due to a dispute over hiring a player from a disbanded team. The All-American Girls Baseball League faded after one dozen seasons in the sun. Their footsteps were unfollowed and, for a time, forgotten.

EXTRA INNINGS

In 1954 there was a long article in the *Racine Journal-Times* about the new activity called Little League baseball. The reporter spoke only to boys and to parents of boys. Although it had been less than five years since Girls Baseball was a part of Racine life, no one asked why girls were not allowed to play Little League, and why newspapers wrote of fathers who would coach the teams while mothers would simply "cheer."

Twenty years later, in 1974, another Racine newspaper article spoke of starting a softball league for fifth- and sixth-grade girls. The brief story mentioned twice that the girls were "enthusiastic but inexperienced," because Racine, like many American towns, had not thought that enough girls would be interested in athletics to make a program worthwhile.

Ten years later still, in 1984, a thirteen-year-old Racine girl had to fight for the chance to pitch for the Racine

County Youth Sports Association. A news article stated that it took an entire year before the girl's coach and her teammates—all boys—granted her respect as a player, instead of as a girl.

• • • •

Merrie Fidler was one of the girls who grew up during the years when girls were not allowed to play Little League. There had been physical education for girls at Fidler's schools in the early 1960s, and she had grown to love sports. But girls did not play the same games as boys, not even in the intramural competitions most schools had by the 1970s. Girls could use only half of the basketball court, while boys played by professional rules. Football, soccer, and baseball were for boys; softball, with its thick, dead ball, was for girls.

Because boys' games were more exciting to watch, more people came to see boys play, and only men had professional teams. As far as Merrie Fidler knew, this was the way things had always been.

Even so, Fidler decided to study physical education. She earned a bachelor's degree, and went on studying for her master's. For this degree, she would have to write a thesis paper, a comprehensive study as long as a book. She wanted to write about women in sports, but not the obvious women famous at the time—tennis players and figure skaters. She wanted to write about women's teams, but she had never heard of any.

Fidler went to the library, hoping to find inspiration. She consulted the *Reader's Guide to Periodical Literature*, which lists magazine articles and authors beginning in the 1940s. Starting with the oldest *Guide*, she saw a curious entry: a 1943 article in *Time* magazine about women playing professional baseball. She had never heard of such a thing.

She looked up the article. It was about an actual League in four midwestern cities—not a traveling barnstorming group, like the turn-of-the-century Bloomer Girls or the Negro League exhibition squads, but a real League with homestands and regular paychecks. But the article talked only of the start of the League. How long had it lasted?

Fidler wrote to the sports editors of the newspapers in each of the four original towns, asking for help researching the Girls Softball League, as it had been called in *Time*. Joe Boland in South Bend wrote back, saying he had been the beat reporter for the South Bend Blue Sox more than twenty years before. He put Fidler in touch with former team manager Chet Grant at Notre Dame, and with Jean Faut, a former Blue Sox pitcher who still lived in South Bend. Because her husband had served on the Blue Sox board of directors, Faut had binders of meeting minutes, news releases, and financial reports that gave Fidler an insider's look at the League's formation.

There were no books Fidler could consult for information, only newspaper clippings and magazine articles, yearbooks and scrapbooks, and memories. She hadn't planned to become a scholarly explorer, but the more she learned, going by word of mouth to find more players and scrapbooks, the more fascinated she became.

Jean Faut's files led Fidler to Arthur Meyerhoff, still maintaining a Chicago office. He was willing to help. He advised her to speak with Philip Wrigley, which she did two years before Wrigley's death in April 1977. No one seemed to have spoken to Wrigley about the Girls League before or after that; newspaper obituaries on Wrigley mentioned nothing about his pioneering work in women's athletics.

So Fidler became the first person to organize information on the Girls League. "I didn't realize at the time I was being a pioneer," she said. "I was just doing my thesis."

The players she met were also pioneers who had not considered themselves as such; they had just been playing the game they loved.

Merrie Fidler's thesis paper was published at the University of Massachussetts in 1976. Such papers are usually photocopied from the student's typewritten manuscript and placed in the university library. The public is often unaware of the treasures within.

• • • •

In 1976, Sharon Roepke had never heard of women playing baseball. When she had graduated from her Michigan high school in 1964, there had been no varsity sports for girls. She now played on an amateur Michigan softball team, and was surprised one day when an elderly gentleman said that her team reminded him of a professional women's baseball team.

Roepke had grown up in Michigan, in the 1950s no less; it seemed strange that, with her love of sports, she had never heard of this. But another fellow said that he had read about a women's league, too, in some old baseball guides. Roepke headed to the library.

She found banner headline newspaper coverage of the local team, but no books. She began asking around to see if anyone from the League was still in the area, finding a player, a coach, and a chaperone. Most had packed their memories into attic trunks. Some had children who didn't know that their own mothers had once played professional ball.

Roepke, who was working as a women's counselor, became more and more curious about the ballplayers who had left a happy part of their lives behind. She contacted the National Baseball Hall of Fame in Cooperstown, New York, to learn more about the League, and she discovered that the Hall had no idea what the Girls League was or that women had ever had a place in American baseball. Roepke decided to change that.

A trip to Cooperstown showed that the library there did possess the old baseball guides, as well as one slim file of clips about women in baseball, primarily team owners. Roepke returned home and began seeking out more players, planning to compile a history of the League that would be easier to read than a stack of clippings. With the fruits of her research, she began making presentations to organizations such as the Society for American Baseball Research and the North American Society of Sports History. Most of the audiences were composed of men. Their enthusiastic response hinted to Roepke that men might make room in the Hall of Fame for the women of the League.

Like any baseball lover, Roepke knew that the Hall was "the Church of Baseball." It enshrines the best and brightest. It tells the story of baseball's evolving importance in American culture. It was, Roepke believed, a place that the Girls League needed to be, so it would not be forgotten again.

She continued to interview players, so many that in 1980, when former Kalamazoo pitcher June Peppas decided to start a newsletter to keep former players in touch, Sharon provided the addresses.

"When that envelope came with the logo of the League," Belles catcher Irene Hickson would say of her first newsletter, "I thought, well, it is spring. Time to get a new player contract!"

• • • •

"The old gray mare, she ain't what she used to be. . . ." Just as they sang together on buses thirty years before, the All-

Americans sang as they gathered for their first reunion in 1982. They sang before their "old-timers" game. They sang in banquet halls.

But the old gray mare hadn't really changed so much. Mischievous as ever, players posted their friends' hotel telephone numbers on posh hotel bulletin boards with the headline "Room Service—All Hours."

Chicago. All-Americans could see the Wrigley Building carving out a piece of summer sky. They would go to Wrigley Field and remember how the Girls League had played a Red Cross benefit game there one night in 1943 under portable lights. In 1982 the field still didn't have lights.

Some memories rushed back; others came slowly. The All-American Girls Baseball League had proved difficult to explain to people who had never seen it. No, it wasn't softball, players repeated. Sometimes they wondered themselves if it had all been real.

Sharon Roepke came to meet the people she knew from reading yellowed newspaper clippings. She interviewed players, and planned a book that would prove the All-American Girls belonged in the National Baseball Hall of Fame.

Some women, she learned, had continued playing baseball after 1954 on a summer tour squad. For three years "Bill Allington's All-Americans" played local amateur men's teams. Switching batteries, so that women pitched to women and men to men, the All-Americans almost always won. But Allington's All-Americans faded after 1957. Life on the road was rough, even for people who loved the game, and the pay for touring teams was unstable.

And so the last All-Americans turned, like their teammates before them, to real estate or journalism or electronics. They operated print shops or drove school buses and cleaning trucks. They taught school, sold insurance, became doctors, joined the Air Force and the police force. Some stayed in athletics. If given the chance, they coached and umpired Little League baseball. They raised families, and taught their children how to play ball.

Helen Callaghan's son, Casey Candaele, grew up to join the major leagues. His mother taught him how to hit.

Joanne Winter became a professional golfer and golf instructor. Karen Kunkel worked to establish women's skiing competitions at United States colleges.

Others couldn't even watch baseball for a number of years. It hurt too much to think there was no longer a place for women in the game.

In 1984, Roepke created her first set of All-American Girls Professional Baseball League baseball cards, using photographs of uniformed All-Americans in their playing days. She tabulated statistics from yearbooks and newspapers, and printed season-by-season totals on the card backs. She continued to give lectures about the Girls League, circulating petitions for recognition of the All-American Girls Professional Baseball League by the National Baseball Hall of Fame. She urged former players to establish an alumni association and present their cause to the Hall with a unified voice.

There was initial resistance from the Hall. Roepke and some former All-Americans believed that the Girls League deserved induction, or official membership, in the Hall. Hall representatives stood by their policy of inducting only individuals who had a major-league career of ten seasons or more. Negro Leaguers were not inducted until 1969, because it was not until then that prewar, all-black teams were recognized by the Hall as a "major" league.

But curator Ted Spencer was intrigued by another unknown chapter of America's pastime. His discovery that his own grade-school physical education instructor, Mary Pratt, was a former All-American helped speed the devel-

*Still rooting for Racine in 1988, Hutch holds
a photo of herself in earlier days.*

opment of a permanent exhibit at the Hall entitled "Women in Baseball."

On November 5, 1988, tourists in Cooperstown, New York, wondered—some even asked—why so many "old ladies" were in town? The answer was that one hundred and fifty members of the Girls League Alumni Association had gathered to see the opening of "their" display at the National Baseball Hall of Fame Museum. Surrounded by friends, families, former students, and grandchildren, All-Americans filled the Hall that autumn afternoon. There was barely room to move or breathe. The excitement of seeing old teammates and opponents was doubled by the fact that they were in Cooperstown.

The Hall of Fame, a respected judge of baseball talent, once recognized only the accomplishments of white men in baseball. Later, men of all races were accepted. In 1988 the Hall acknowledged women's deserved place in sports history.

The exhibit features more than the players of the All-American League. Umpire Pam Postema and Cincinnati Reds owner Marge Schott are some of the other women included. But the majority of the display is devoted to the Girls League. Photos of players, an actual uniform, the varying sizes of balls, bats, and other equipment are all exhibited in the center of the showcase. Most important, a list names the 545 participants who played professional girls baseball. Every All-American Girl is now a part of American history.

A small showcase on the second floor of a remote, small-town museum is perhaps the biggest monument the All-Americans will ever receive. It affirms that, no matter what the score might have been on a sticky summer evening in Kalamazoo, every member of the All-American Girls Professional Baseball League was, and remains, a winner.

GIRLS LEAGUE
HISTORY

1942   Philip K. Wrigley invents the idea of a baseball league for women.

1944   Name of All-American Girls Softball League is changed to All-American Girls Professional Baseball League.

1945   World War II ends. Arthur Meyerhoff assumes control of the League.

1946   Ball size reduced to 11 inches. Sidearm pitching allowed. Racine wins second League championship. Sophie Kurys steals 201 bases, a modern record. Juniors teams formed.

1947   Pitchers required to throw sidearm. Spring training is held in Cuba.

1948   Pitchers adopt overhand motions. New teams form in Chicago (Colleens) and Springfield (Sallies). Each fails at year's end. League conducts exhibition tour in South America.

1949   League switches to 10-inch ball.

1950   Final season for Racine and Muskegon teams, marking first established teams to close due to financial problems.

1951   Private groups buy individual teams from Meyerhoff.

1954   League changes to regulation baseball and 85-foot basepaths. Five surviving teams disband, ending the life of the All-American Girls Professional Baseball League.

1976   Student Merrie Fidler writes a 374-page college thesis on the history of the forgotten League.

1980   Former player June Peppas begins publishing a newsletter for other members of the League.

1982   Remaining members of the League hold first national reunion.

1988   A "Women in Baseball" exhibit is created in the National Baseball Hall of Fame in Cooperstown, New York, honoring the Girls League.

CITIES FEATURING ALL-AMERICAN GIRLS LEAGUE TEAMS

City	Team	Years
Rockford, Illinois	Peaches	1943–1954
South Bend, Indiana	Blue Sox	1943–1954
Kenosha, Wisconsin	Comets	1943–1951
Racine, Wisconsin	Belles	1943–1950
Milwaukee, Wisconsin	Chicks	1944
Minneapolis, Minnesota	Millerettes	1944
Grand Rapids, Michigan	Chicks	1945–1954
Fort Wayne, Indiana	Daisies	1945–1954
Muskegon, Michigan	Lassies	1946–1950
Peoria, Illinois	Redwings	1946–1951
Chicago, Illinois	Colleens	1948
Springfield, Illinois	Sallies	1948
Kalamazoo, Michigan	Lassies	1950–1954
Battle Creek, Michigan	Belles	1951–1952
Muskegon, Michigan	Belles	1953

SELECTED
BIBLIOGRAPHY

Cahn, Susan M. "No Freaks, No Amazons, No Boyish Bobs." *Chicago History Magazine*, Spring 1989.

Feldman, Jay. "Glamour Ball." *Sports Heritage Magazine*, May/June 1987.

Fidler, Merrie A. "The Development and Decline of the All-American Girls Baseball League, 1943–1954." University of Massachusetts thesis, 1976.

Fincher, Jack. "The Belles of the Ball Game Were a Hit with Their Fans." *Smithsonian Magazine*, July 1989.

Major League Baseball 1944 (also 1945–1949 editions), Dell Publishing, 1944–49.

Roepke, Sharon L. *Diamond Gals—The Story of the All-American Girls Professional Baseball League*. AAGBL Cards, 1986.

Wilson, Kim, and Candaele, Kelly. *A League of Their Own*. Documentary, Filmmakers Library, New York.

AUTHOR'S NOTE

This is sure to be an incomplete litany of those who helped with the research of this book. These people and more deserve many thanks: Anna May Hutchison and Gladys Day for their loving hospitality; Joyce Hill Westerman and her husband, Ray, for sharing memories, time, and scrapbooks; likewise, Anastasia "Stash" Batikis, Norman "Nummy" Derringer, Herb Hoppe, Marie "Blackie" Wegman, and the valiant Irene "Choo-Choo" Hickson.

There were countless Racine citizens who went out of their ways, including the staffs of the Racine Public Library and the Racine and Kenosha historical societies, Heather Black Egan, Janet Wells Raffini, Mary Willmes, Beth Johnson, Diane Giles, Paul Douglas, and Pearl Jorgensen. Redwings fans were wonderful, too: Jacques Katus and Norm Westerdahl. Members of the Society for American Baseball Research sent generous articles and letters of support. Ray Medeiros and Lee Smith gave of their photographic expertise. Woody English and Casey Candaele took the time to provide insightful interviews.

The ground-breaking works of Merrie Fidler and Sharon Roepke were invaluable. Their willingness to share their labors and their own memories is greatly appreciated.

Photos courtesy of Diana Helmer: pp. 3, 86; Anna May Hutchison: pp. 15, 32 (bottom left), 35 (top), 41 (top), 43 (top), 44, 57 (top), 65 (bottom); Racine County Historical Society and Museum, Inc.: p. 32 (top and bottom right), 35 (bottom), 41 (bottom); National Baseball Library, Cooperstown, NY: p. 43 (bottom); Joyce Hill Westerman: p. 46, 50 (both), 57 (bottom), 58 (both), 65 (top and center); Herb Hoppe: p. 71.

INDEX

Page numbers in *italics* refer to illustrations.

796.357 Helmer, Diana Star.
HEL
         Belles of the
          ballpark.

$16.40   2958

DATE